HIGHWAY SUITE

HIGHWAY SUITE

Emily Warn

Limberlost Press
1988

ACKNOWLEDGEMENTS

Special thanks to the editors of the following magazines
where some of these poems first appeared: *Hubbub, Seattle
Image, The Slackwater Review, Crabcreek Review, Cauldron,
Poetry NOW, Backbone, The Seattle Review, Rhino,*
and *The Limberlost Review.*

Limberlost Press
Rick & Rosemary Ardinger, Editors
HC 33, Box 1113
Boise, Idaho 83706

CONTENTS

For Ellen Cooper

Highway Suite

Leaving again,
my car drones up the pass,
drifts in and out of fog
before climbing steeply up toward treeline.
Each time I travel through the pass
a change occurs,
as the rain-fed,
rain-gorged,
lush green blossoming
of moss and mold gives way
to white slopes of snow.
It is like the moment
after I say goodbye,
or like reaching the silt of the shallows
after a long swim and a rest,
after a dive into the mind's solitary waters:
rest   dive   and   change
and in the instance of change forget
who we think we are
and become ourselves for a slow moment
I want to lengthen between us.

Cipher

The Sawtooth pyramids rise along the highway,
the first interesting signs
after the endless white flatlands
of Washington, Oregon and Idaho.
Even the sage gone,
last year's scrub blown to the edge
where it walled against a house
that transmits silence. No static.
No wavering cowboy tunes,
or the last seconds of the fourth quarter
fading in and out across the plains.
Simply blank space, a quiet corner,
where I can turn to listen,
not to wind driving snow across stubble,
or the blink of neon at the "all-night" gas station,
but simple interstellar quiet. The kind I imagine
looking past the fixed stars, or when I am lost
in heavy fog or snow and every direction is white.
In front of me, a diesel gears down
so the rear wheels won't slip
off the thread of road that leads
to home, where a shelf in a pantry is loaded
with jams and old bottles of wine,
where in the safety of the kitchen lamp,
I open the sealed goods of a previous life.

Poem for My Students in Hailey, Idaho

Like the last pages of a Russian novel,
the snow is falling, thick, fast,
dimming until we think it is evening,
the day done, nothing to do but stare
at the vanishing act. The knuckled hills
and sky blur into white. The sloped roofs
and cars are half-gone into cloudy impressions.
We pause in our lesson,
watching ourselves disappear
and reappear as we bring
what is outside in.
When the snow plows arrive
with their yellow insect lights,
let the words of this poem
finish the snow's drifting form.

Johnson's Orchards

The pewter-grey apple trees
cannot lose themselves in the fog.
They call to each other,
a slight clack of their clipped branches,
a slight tip of their frozen chalices
rippling up the perfect rows.
In their tended order, they are beautiful:
grafted from cultured stock,
shaped to hold sunlight in their palms.
They are the orchardist's desire
for a safe journey.
In the white dawn,
a few yellow kitchen lights,
spaced far apart on the winter roads, flick on;
a few cars strafe the snow.
Soon the troops of pickups
and high school hotrods pass,
feeding the fog their headlights,
to work, to school, to swear
at the clock rule.
But for a time,
under the brief coffee spell
in the cold front seat,
the radio crackle warming the air,
we are free.
Lulled by the hypnotic flash of furrowed trees,
we speed past the hay racks,
past the stacked apple bins
which will outlast us
as we fade towards the ground,
where the apple trees are rooted,
stiff, sturdy, waving at the sky.

Winter Pruning

Later today, I will prune the apple trees.
I will not be happy as I am now,
warmed by one last fire of winter,
irresponsible and alone as those apple wands
in their yearly run towards the sky,
before I snag them, clip them back to one knuckle,
one hard bud that will bear red, sweet fruit.
Would those sky-ambling shoots—if I didn't stop them—
bend, eventually, in a graceful arc like willows
whose long yellow strands guide the eye down
to a glassy pond, where their tear-shaped leaves
mingle with the sky?
If I let the shoots ramble, untrained,
their fruit would soften, shrink in size.
Their yearly run, then, is like our daily run
toward pleasure—the pleasure of food
or sleep that we check in order to make our lives.
In front of the fire, I think with pleasure
of pruning the apple trees, but when I climb the ladder,
balanced by rung and lopper, and let the curving blade
find the base of last year's growth
and snip off all but one or two buds,
I'll worry about the angle of the cut,
about disturbing fifteen-year-old spurs,
about how much sunlight and wind
to allow into the center.
I'll worry that all my clipping and thinning,
all my worrying and puzzling,
has not found the perfect shape of the tree.
I will not be happy.
It is much easier to sit
by a fire I don't really need,
to reflect like the willow
about the apple, to be as useless
as those wands, those star-straining rods.

Kahlotus, Washington

Name the landmarks of this town:
Windust Park. Devil's Canyon Road.
The shacks by Kahlotus Lake.
Tom's Cafe. Compare memories.
Begin with a word, any word, like erasure.
Forget what you know of poetry.
Tell me something about yourself,
something no one else here knows.
View your life from the mammoth, chalky "K"
whitewashed on the hill behind the schoolyard.
Step outside yourself, as you do,
driving the desert roads,
the future momentarily lit
then swallowed by headlights.
The roads cut half-moons, ellipses
out of the wave motion of the land,
an endless plateau of dirt farms, dryland wheat fields,
unfenced, beyond reach of human feet.

Mainstreet Kahlotus is fixed up like the old west—
wooden sidewalks, false fronts, a jailhouse—
all dwarfed by the huge grain elevator.
No one remembers the facades or the rusting jail.

I drive the Devil's Canyon Road,
a steep grade down, a channel cut by the Snake
through a tabletop of wheat and sage.
At dusk, the faint green relief of young winter wheat
disappears; the land smothers the sky, and there is nothing
but headlights illuminating a future
notched by mile markers between small ranch towns.

Double J Ranch

Cattails buzz with blackbirds,
last year's fluff, this year's song.
Sun, at last, widening the sky mirrors
at the rim of the pond,
where the ice melts,
where the cattails stand twice.
I curl in the hay,
absent myself from friends.
Clouds one after another cross the plateau.
By evening I will not speak.
Refrain after refrain of blackbirds, meadowlark,
Great Horned Owl in the aspen grove behind the barn.
Sun, warm away my need for comfort, my restraint.
Not sure what eats at me.
Barren sea of last year's grass.

Johnny's Cafe

The waitress remembers Philip Levine
when he worked his string of stupid jobs
in Detroit. I was about to be born
in the first white suburb.
Soon as I could
I rode the Woodward bus downtown.
From our door in a row of apartments,
it was one long mile past the Rackman Golf Course
and the Detroit Zoo to the stop.
The lions roared when they fed them
at five a.m. and woke us cursing them
and the cold snowy walk to school.
The golf course froze in winter.
Occasional peacocks and ring-neck pheasants escaped
and strolled on the iced over pond at the ninth hole,
their clipped wings bent after a wind
that would carry them to a coast,
any coast where the wind catches and flaps,
where I've walked and thrown my life at the edge
knowing it would return unharmed
and full-bodied as the tides
crusted with fragments of shellfish and salt.
The rock salt they throw on Woodward Avenue
rusts the bodies of cars as quick
as factories forge them;
factories where Philip Levine threw his life
after a dollar. It came back empty and starved
for something no one can find in Detroit,
but everywhere its absence hints louder
than the sea with all its watery, dramatic sighs.

Logging Road

Quick strides. Late.
The hazy grey mist shadowed black
as the dark pines. The rain just over,
loosened its hold after seven days.
Conduit pipes rushing, creeks full,
torrents of brown muddy rivulets
hidden by knotted ditch grass.
Water seeps out of the mud banks,
cedar feathers breathe,
branches shake, quiver whole, sigh.
No longer separate, huddled inside,
a dog barks, loud, insistent, disturbing.
Continual flow of footsteps and water forward,
running off the slopes into the creek
untangling passages, think.

Border Town

The Pend Oreille flows past, smooth, slow, wide
in the windows of the Box Canyon Motel.
On the far bank, Canadian geese and juncos
trill and honk. A train floats in,
its whistle loud and sharp.
In the quiet, everyone notices the wildlife,
or seems to in their boasts of sixteen elk
in the field by Lowe's farm at dusk,
or three mountain goats on the rock face
above Harry's creek, feeding its ghostly blue
glacier water into the Pend Oreille,
pronounced *Ponderey*—good American English
spoken by a handful of locals moored inside
the riverwalls of cedar, larch and fir.
They hung on after the mine closed,
after the mill shut down.
The cement plant hums—
eighty-six years of limestone mountain chewed.
Four men work the old zinc mine,
running the pumps, pushing water out
of the maze of underground roads.

For what reason do people patch together lives here?
One eye is on the woodpile, the other on weather,
hands hard at work, steaming coffee or making soup.
The cement plant dusts the boarded-up stores
with fine white sand.
Soon the mine workers will open the gates,
flood the underground tunnels and leave.
Quietly, the river slides by,
green with limestone, blue with glacial melt.
Quietly, the people drive up and down,
twelve miles between two tiny towns.
Their numbers rise and fall
with each rumor about the mill.

Postcard from Sun Valley

It's spring again.
The perfect hills, faint green, rise
in the sun. I sort through your dream
of faith in a hopeless world.
You kept turning your face
toward other faces and death.
A flock of birds picks at seeds
under the matted grass
weighted all winter by snow.
These birds never heard of Seattle,
its months and months of regret,
how the rain postpones living forever.
The flowers, though, make you forget
despair. I miss them here.
No ripe pink azaleas climbing the rockery
for a shiney view of the lake.
No tulips, no crocus, no sweet lilac smell.
Here the grey-green sage scours
the already clean, treeless air, meaning:
Step out into the sun.
Open the door.
Here's my chance to dream
a place in the grass,
a broken mat of sticks and sage.
Tiny lilies shield me from myself.

Pastoral

It is simple to tell
how I scooted—killdeer-like—past the cattails,
how I climbed the desert bluffs—green with winter rains,
yellow with balsam flower—swift and keen as a meadowlark,
pausing to trill at each rock
embedded in the sparse soil,
And then I slowed,
slowed the wing beat of my heart,
slowed the endless ripple of thought,
until I blinked in time to the green ridge illumined
after each passing cloud,
until I drank from the pasture creek
level with the mushroom grass and sky.
Slowed until I mimicked the movement
of willows with my breath,
slowed past doubt and ecstasy,
and then entered the cropped pasture,
to walk invisibly among the black and russet cows.

Reflection

Happiness. The sun actually dawned.
The world a mess of fog steaming blue.
I want you with me this morning.
The quartz clock ticks efficiently.
Student papers sorted in piles.
Your hipsockets my belly.
I'm far away in the wettest corner of Washington:
Greys Harbor. I watch wind tufts of rain
sweep over the flowing marsh grasses;
sandpipers rise and swerve, flipping in unison.
Buffeted and scattered, they rejoin
in the shallow salty puddles,
in the long grass invisible
this longing to join you.
We could mimic the loon's dive
into the ruffled harbor waters,
re-appear implausibly calm.

Yakima River Valley

Last year's cattails hush and clatter at the diesel
lumbering past the irrigation ditches.
Here in the heartland, fields are brushed blue by the sky.
The land is spaced evenly with homesteads;
people know one another and stay clear.
I feel afraid at the creak of cowboy boots,
at the stiff talk over coffee at highway cafes.

The river pots wide bends with alder and cottonwood.
Their leaves tremble with water
above the grazed land and planked barns.
In their shadows, cows ramble to river water,
erode the banks as they pick their way
past trucks rusting in the willows.
From my perch, I stoop and bend like a weighted branch,
nod with each tick of the current,
fill my heart with river stones.

What we want is always here.
What we don't know will find us
if the roadside cattails nod
to us and we listen.
If we looked, we could find words
that contain the space of this old river delta:
opaque blue, transparent blue.
Worlds could pass between us like river sounds,
like the silver of the current
if we let them.

Rubber Soul

Damn. I've been reading Hugo again
and like a two-bit poet in a bar some place
I soak up the juice and deliver,
certain I hit on the meaning of the moment
or the universe depending on my scope.
Of course, nothing's certain
but these goddamned selves
that are slow to change or never do
except for us, when we write a poem,
or for me, when it's morning again and I slept.
Then the world is as fresh
as a thin band of shadows
from skinny poplars lining a country road,
their leaves yellow as apples. An easy simile.
I think my imagination is worn to shreds
from teaching poetry. In French, apple sounds
like how I say poem in my middle western accent
that swallows words to keep
what is secret about Michigan soil,
carp buried in fields for next year's crop.
There, I've given some of it away,
like I did last night
when I read the poem to my father
to a junior high crowd. Kids respond to real emotion.
For another poem, I had to explain the Sixties,
how we played Beatle albums backward
to find out the lyrics' true meaning.
There's a composer here who can do that,
recite words backward so that when played forward
they sound like the real thing.
Let's both keep trying.

La Push Ocean Park

The Quileute woman we met had come to check
her gill net anchored to the spotted river rocks.
According to Indian law, her net floated
one-third the width of the river,
buoyed by corks, held down by lead weights
and salmon caught in the netting.
Her family has fished here for generations.
She named the men on the far side of river,
pointed out the tribal school (an old clapboard
Coast Guard Station), and the three fishhouses
where she sold her catch.
We peered in at the tribal center,
at its totems and Fisheries' posters,
walked past dilapidated houses
and fixed-up quaint houses,
and muffler-dragging cars set against
a backdrop of sea and harbor mast.

The Quileute believed they died into an underworld
where they waited until spring to don salmon skins
and begin the yearly run past boulder and waterfall
to spawn. Human beings mirroring nature,
beliefs that wove the living skein of the planet.
I wanted to ask that woman if she still believes
even though a handful of white men
dammed the path of the sea-running salmon.
Behind us, we heard the boom and lull of the sea.
Brown Pelicans circled the off shore sea stacks—
remnants of islands, immovable.
Three children leaned out of her idling Chevrolet
laughing and impatient that she took so long
telling strangers the price of salmon.

Outpost

A family climbs down through sage.
Soon, they'll enter the wooded river bottom.
I watch, a hawk on a weathered log,
an empty soul, waiting
for the loud snow melt flooded creek
to tell me something.
Meadowlark skitter,
a flock of brown birds, scared.
Alone here, really alone.

Okanogan Plateau

We walk the fence line,
crisscrossing fields of ripening wheat
and dusty clods of summer fallow.
On the far horizon,
mountains stop the endless sky.
Our path drops beneath a bluff
and we are stunned by still water,
by a flock of gulls in the shadow of cliffs
rising from the far side of a marshy lake.

A slight breeze rattles the aspen.
We lie naked in the shore grass
under a hot sun and porcelain blue sky.
The cliffs, streaked with lichen,
tell a prehistory that we join
as we enter the black water,
scattering water spiders and silt.
Our voices echo off the cliffs, startle us,
so we swim silently, languidly on our backs
or flip over and part the surface like beaver.
In the heat of afternoon, we doze off,
until wakened by the cries of gulls.
The sun sinking behind the cliffs
quiets our conversation.
Aware of our bodies,
of the sea birds cricling,
we rise dreamily as dragon flies
hovering above the glassy water.

Artichoke

The long frond-like leaves
turned yellow in August,
the fruit still ripening, we thought,
on the stalk. Instead it blossomed.
Now each time I eat the pulpy leaves,
I'll think of the purple spikes,
like a thistle or sea urchin,
like the inner petals clamped
around the artichoke's heart have opened.

Oh, I know,
     the last chord strummed will fade,
     the melodic voice bow
     to the click of the arm,
     the turntable circle to a stop.

We listen, poised
     to break silence with a look.
     We hesitate to speak,
     to shape any questions.

     Brush of wool as we sip coffee.
     Rain in the streets.

        I want to hear your voice
        reveal something I need to know.
        I want to tell you how much
        I learn by listening.

We press against each other,
     unfasten each button,
     trust the silence of breath
        as we collide,
        the arpeggio of desire spoken.

Labor Day

Today is the last day of summer.
Nothing and no one moves.
A slight breeze nods the boats
drifting in pontoons on the bay.
On the shore we are just as lazy,
stationed on the grass for the best view.
We brought our picnics and novels
to bury our goals before autumn begins.

If I glance at the lake, at the water
lapping the sides of fiberglass boats,
I lose the rhythm of thought
and am back at a lake outside Detroit,
the shallows littered with rusty pipes
that we empty looking for crayfish or frogs.
We circle the shore, swim under piers,
chase the glint of sunfish shells,
anything that lets us endlessly search
like minnows gleaming in and out of the weeds.
When we come to an opening,
where the seawall has cracked,
where water crawls up on shore and rests,
we rest, then explore further
until hunger forces us home.

Today it is this memory and the idea of memory
that creates a space larger than the lake
to mesmerize me, allows me to forget
the momentum of years, and I am as yet unformed,
faceless as the girl who drifted along the shore
unaware the days shifted away from the sun.

An Empty Word

*In Chinese poetry, a character that has
no meaning in itself, but serves to move
the narrative along, to allow the story
to continue.*

The rain continues its limitless song.
The tap tap   tap percusses the roof,
      rotten beams there,
here the whole notes of sound timbers.
Finger tips of rain,
someone lost in thought,
or a snare drum left in the wind,
    a bell hung in an estuary
    to sound something human
    among the tall geese and wavering reeds.

Between the apple trees,
the empty yard is drenched.
I listen to the wind prepare the ear for silence,
to the wind carrying the breath of a hundred prayers.
    Wide marsh
    Deep throated birds
    Flutes over water